MW01037726

Password Book

****

NAME
PHONE
CELL
EMAIL

STREET
CITY, STATE, ZIP
COUNTRY

WI-FI NETWORK
PASSWORD

WEBSITE
USERNAME
PASSWORD
NOTES

WEBSITE
USERNAME
PASSWORD
NOTES

WEBSITE
USERNAME
PASSWORD
NOTES

WEBSITE
USERNAME
PASSWORD
NOTES

WEBSITE
USERNAME
PASSWORD
NOTES

••

WEBSITE
USERNAME
PASSWORD
NOTES

••

WEBSITE
USERNAME
PASSWORD
NOTES

••

WEBSITE
USERNAME
PASSWORD
NOTES

WEBSITE

USERNAME

PASSWORD

NOTES

....

WEBSITE

USERNAME

PASSWORD

NOTES

....

WEBSITE

USERNAME

PASSWORD

NOTES

....

WEBSITE

USERNAME

PASSWORD

NOTES

WEBSITE

USERNAME

PASSWORD

NOTES

· ·

WEBSITE

USERNAME

PASSWORD

NOTES

· ·

WEBSITE

USERNAME

PASSWORD

NOTES

· ·

WEBSITE

USERNAME

PASSWORD

NOTES

B

WEBSITE
_____
USERNAME
_____
PASSWORD
_____
NOTES
_____
_____
_____

•••

WEBSITE
_____
USERNAME
_____
PASSWORD
_____
NOTES
_____
_____
_____

•••

WEBSITE
_____
USERNAME
_____
PASSWORD
_____
NOTES
_____
_____
_____

•••

WEBSITE
_____
USERNAME
_____
PASSWORD
_____
NOTES
_____
_____
_____

WEBSITE

USERNAME

PASSWORD

NOTES

....

WEBSITE

USERNAME

PASSWORD

NOTES

....

WEBSITE

USERNAME

PASSWORD

NOTES

....

WEBSITE

USERNAME

PASSWORD

NOTES

WEBSITE
USERNAME
PASSWORD
NOTES

....
WEBSITE
USERNAME
PASSWORD
NOTES

....
WEBSITE
USERNAME
PASSWORD
NOTES

....
WEBSITE
USERNAME
PASSWORD
NOTES

WEBSITE
USERNAME
PASSWORD
NOTES

....

WEBSITE
USERNAME
PASSWORD
NOTES

....

WEBSITE
USERNAME
PASSWORD
NOTES

....

WEBSITE
USERNAME
PASSWORD
NOTES

WEBSITE

USERNAME

PASSWORD

NOTES

· ·

WEBSITE

USERNAME

PASSWORD

NOTES

· ·

WEBSITE

USERNAME

PASSWORD

NOTES

· ·

WEBSITE

USERNAME

PASSWORD

NOTES

WEBSITE

USERNAME

PASSWORD

NOTES

....

WEBSITE

USERNAME

PASSWORD

NOTES

....

WEBSITE

USERNAME

PASSWORD

NOTES

....

WEBSITE

USERNAME

PASSWORD

NOTES

WEBSITE
USERNAME
PASSWORD
NOTES

••

WEBSITE
USERNAME
PASSWORD
NOTES

••

WEBSITE
USERNAME
PASSWORD
NOTES

••

WEBSITE
USERNAME
PASSWORD
NOTES

WEBSITE

USERNAME

PASSWORD

NOTES

··

WEBSITE

USERNAME

PASSWORD

NOTES

··

WEBSITE

USERNAME

PASSWORD

NOTES

··

WEBSITE

USERNAME

PASSWORD

NOTES

WEBSITE
USERNAME
PASSWORD
NOTES

WEBSITE
USERNAME
PASSWORD
NOTES

WEBSITE
USERNAME
PASSWORD
NOTES

WEBSITE
USERNAME
PASSWORD
NOTES

WEBSITE
USERNAME
PASSWORD
NOTES

··

WEBSITE
USERNAME
PASSWORD
NOTES

··

WEBSITE
USERNAME
PASSWORD
NOTES

··

WEBSITE
USERNAME
PASSWORD
NOTES

WEBSITE
USERNAME
PASSWORD
NOTES

....
WEBSITE
USERNAME
PASSWORD
NOTES

....
WEBSITE
USERNAME
PASSWORD
NOTES

....
WEBSITE
USERNAME
PASSWORD
NOTES

WEBSITE
USERNAME
PASSWORD
NOTES

....
WEBSITE
USERNAME
PASSWORD
NOTES

....
WEBSITE
USERNAME
PASSWORD
NOTES

....
WEBSITE
USERNAME
PASSWORD
NOTES

WEBSITE
USERNAME
PASSWORD
NOTES

....

WEBSITE
USERNAME
PASSWORD
NOTES

....

WEBSITE
USERNAME
PASSWORD
NOTES

....

WEBSITE
USERNAME
PASSWORD
NOTES

WEBSITE
USERNAME
PASSWORD
NOTES

....
WEBSITE
USERNAME
PASSWORD
NOTES

....
WEBSITE
USERNAME
PASSWORD
NOTES

....
WEBSITE
USERNAME
PASSWORD
NOTES

WEBSITE

USERNAME

PASSWORD

NOTES

· ·

WEBSITE

USERNAME

PASSWORD

NOTES

· ·

WEBSITE

USERNAME

PASSWORD

NOTES

· ·

WEBSITE

USERNAME

PASSWORD

NOTES

WEBSITE
USERNAME
PASSWORD
NOTES

....

WEBSITE
USERNAME
PASSWORD
NOTES

....

WEBSITE
USERNAME
PASSWORD
NOTES

....

WEBSITE
USERNAME
PASSWORD
NOTES

WEBSITE

USERNAME

PASSWORD

NOTES

· ·

WEBSITE

USERNAME

PASSWORD

NOTES

· ·

WEBSITE

USERNAME

PASSWORD

NOTES

· ·

WEBSITE

USERNAME

PASSWORD

NOTES

WEBSITE

USERNAME

PASSWORD

NOTES

....

WEBSITE

USERNAME

PASSWORD

NOTES

....

WEBSITE

USERNAME

PASSWORD

NOTES

....

WEBSITE

USERNAME

PASSWORD

NOTES

WEBSITE
USERNAME
PASSWORD
NOTES

....

WEBSITE
USERNAME
PASSWORD
NOTES

....

WEBSITE
USERNAME
PASSWORD
NOTES

....

WEBSITE
USERNAME
PASSWORD
NOTES

WEBSITE

USERNAME

PASSWORD

NOTES

....

WEBSITE

USERNAME

PASSWORD

NOTES

....

WEBSITE

USERNAME

PASSWORD

NOTES

....

WEBSITE

USERNAME

PASSWORD

NOTES

WEBSITE

USERNAME

PASSWORD

NOTES

....

WEBSITE

USERNAME

PASSWORD

NOTES

....

WEBSITE

USERNAME

PASSWORD

NOTES

....

WEBSITE

USERNAME

PASSWORD

NOTES

WEBSITE

USERNAME

PASSWORD

NOTES

....

WEBSITE

USERNAME

PASSWORD

NOTES

....

WEBSITE

USERNAME

PASSWORD

NOTES

....

WEBSITE

USERNAME

PASSWORD

NOTES

WEBSITE

USERNAME

PASSWORD

NOTES

· ·

WEBSITE

USERNAME

PASSWORD

NOTES

· ·

WEBSITE

USERNAME

PASSWORD

NOTES

· ·

WEBSITE

USERNAME

PASSWORD

NOTES

WEBSITE
USERNAME
PASSWORD
NOTES

....
WEBSITE
USERNAME
PASSWORD
NOTES

....
WEBSITE
USERNAME
PASSWORD
NOTES

....
WEBSITE
USERNAME
PASSWORD
NOTES

WEBSITE
USERNAME
PASSWORD
NOTES

WEBSITE
USERNAME
PASSWORD
NOTES

WEBSITE
USERNAME
PASSWORD
NOTES

WEBSITE
USERNAME
PASSWORD
NOTES

WEBSITE
USERNAME
PASSWORD
NOTES

....

WEBSITE
USERNAME
PASSWORD
NOTES

....

WEBSITE
USERNAME
PASSWORD
NOTES

....

WEBSITE
USERNAME
PASSWORD
NOTES

WEBSITE
USERNAME
PASSWORD
NOTES

....

WEBSITE
USERNAME
PASSWORD
NOTES

....

WEBSITE
USERNAME
PASSWORD
NOTES

....

WEBSITE
USERNAME
PASSWORD
NOTES

WEBSITE
USERNAME
PASSWORD
NOTES

· ·

WEBSITE
USERNAME
PASSWORD
NOTES

· ·

WEBSITE
USERNAME
PASSWORD
NOTES

· ·

WEBSITE
USERNAME
PASSWORD
NOTES

WEBSITE
USERNAME
PASSWORD
NOTES

....

WEBSITE
USERNAME
PASSWORD
NOTES

....

WEBSITE
USERNAME
PASSWORD
NOTES

....

WEBSITE
USERNAME
PASSWORD
NOTES

WEBSITE

USERNAME

PASSWORD

NOTES

· ·

WEBSITE

USERNAME

PASSWORD

NOTES

· ·

WEBSITE

USERNAME

PASSWORD

NOTES

· ·

WEBSITE

USERNAME

PASSWORD

NOTES

WEBSITE
USERNAME
PASSWORD
NOTES

....

WEBSITE
USERNAME
PASSWORD
NOTES

....

WEBSITE
USERNAME
PASSWORD
NOTES

....

WEBSITE
USERNAME
PASSWORD
NOTES

WEBSITE

USERNAME

PASSWORD

NOTES

··

WEBSITE

USERNAME

PASSWORD

NOTES

··

WEBSITE

USERNAME

PASSWORD

NOTES

··

WEBSITE

USERNAME

PASSWORD

NOTES

WEBSITE
USERNAME
PASSWORD
NOTES

WEBSITE
USERNAME
PASSWORD
NOTES

WEBSITE
USERNAME
PASSWORD
NOTES

WEBSITE
USERNAME
PASSWORD
NOTES

WEBSITE
USERNAME
PASSWORD
NOTES

··

WEBSITE
USERNAME
PASSWORD
NOTES

··

WEBSITE
USERNAME
PASSWORD
NOTES

··

WEBSITE
USERNAME
PASSWORD
NOTES

WEBSITE

USERNAME

PASSWORD

NOTES

....

WEBSITE

USERNAME

PASSWORD

NOTES

....

WEBSITE

USERNAME

PASSWORD

NOTES

....

WEBSITE

USERNAME

PASSWORD

NOTES

WEBSITE
USERNAME
PASSWORD
NOTES

· ·

WEBSITE
USERNAME
PASSWORD
NOTES

· ·

WEBSITE
USERNAME
PASSWORD
NOTES

· ·

WEBSITE
USERNAME
PASSWORD
NOTES

WEBSITE

USERNAME

PASSWORD

NOTES

....

WEBSITE

USERNAME

PASSWORD

NOTES

....

WEBSITE

USERNAME

PASSWORD

NOTES

....

WEBSITE

USERNAME

PASSWORD

NOTES

WEBSITE

USERNAME

PASSWORD

NOTES

....

WEBSITE

USERNAME

PASSWORD

NOTES

....

WEBSITE

USERNAME

PASSWORD

NOTES

....

WEBSITE

USERNAME

PASSWORD

NOTES

WEBSITE
USERNAME
PASSWORD
NOTES

WEBSITE
USERNAME
PASSWORD
NOTES

WEBSITE
USERNAME
PASSWORD
NOTES

WEBSITE
USERNAME
PASSWORD
NOTES

WEBSITE
USERNAME
PASSWORD
NOTES

WEBSITE
USERNAME
PASSWORD
NOTES

WEBSITE
USERNAME
PASSWORD
NOTES

WEBSITE
USERNAME
PASSWORD
NOTES

WEBSITE
USERNAME
PASSWORD
NOTES

....

WEBSITE
USERNAME
PASSWORD
NOTES

....

WEBSITE
USERNAME
PASSWORD
NOTES

....

WEBSITE
USERNAME
PASSWORD
NOTES

WEBSITE
USERNAME
PASSWORD
NOTES

· ·

WEBSITE
USERNAME
PASSWORD
NOTES

· ·

WEBSITE
USERNAME
PASSWORD
NOTES

· ·

WEBSITE
USERNAME
PASSWORD
NOTES

WEBSITE _____

USERNAME _____

PASSWORD _____

NOTES _____

_____

_____

••

WEBSITE _____

USERNAME _____

PASSWORD _____

NOTES _____

_____

_____

••

WEBSITE _____

USERNAME _____

PASSWORD _____

NOTES _____

_____

_____

••

WEBSITE _____

USERNAME _____

PASSWORD _____

NOTES _____

_____

_____

WEBSITE
USERNAME
PASSWORD
NOTES

....

WEBSITE
USERNAME
PASSWORD
NOTES

....

WEBSITE
USERNAME
PASSWORD
NOTES

....

WEBSITE
USERNAME
PASSWORD
NOTES

WEBSITE
USERNAME
PASSWORD
NOTES

WEBSITE
USERNAME
PASSWORD
NOTES

WEBSITE
USERNAME
PASSWORD
NOTES

WEBSITE
USERNAME
PASSWORD
NOTES

WEBSITE
USERNAME
PASSWORD
NOTES

....

WEBSITE
USERNAME
PASSWORD
NOTES

....

WEBSITE
USERNAME
PASSWORD
NOTES

....

WEBSITE
USERNAME
PASSWORD
NOTES

WEBSITE
USERNAME
PASSWORD
NOTES

....

WEBSITE
USERNAME
PASSWORD
NOTES

....

WEBSITE
USERNAME
PASSWORD
NOTES

....

WEBSITE
USERNAME
PASSWORD
NOTES

WEBSITE
USERNAME
PASSWORD
NOTES

....

WEBSITE
USERNAME
PASSWORD
NOTES

....

WEBSITE
USERNAME
PASSWORD
NOTES

....

WEBSITE
USERNAME
PASSWORD
NOTES

WEBSITE
USERNAME
PASSWORD
NOTES

....

WEBSITE
USERNAME
PASSWORD
NOTES

....

WEBSITE
USERNAME
PASSWORD
NOTES

....

WEBSITE
USERNAME
PASSWORD
NOTES

WEBSITE
USERNAME
PASSWORD
NOTES

....

WEBSITE
USERNAME
PASSWORD
NOTES

....

WEBSITE
USERNAME
PASSWORD
NOTES

....

WEBSITE
USERNAME
PASSWORD
NOTES

WEBSITE

USERNAME

PASSWORD

NOTES

····································

WEBSITE

USERNAME

PASSWORD

NOTES

····································

WEBSITE

USERNAME

PASSWORD

NOTES

····································

WEBSITE

USERNAME

PASSWORD

NOTES

WEBSITE
USERNAME
PASSWORD
NOTES

WEBSITE
USERNAME
PASSWORD
NOTES

WEBSITE
USERNAME
PASSWORD
NOTES

WEBSITE
USERNAME
PASSWORD
NOTES

WEBSITE
USERNAME
PASSWORD
NOTES

....

WEBSITE
USERNAME
PASSWORD
NOTES

....

WEBSITE
USERNAME
PASSWORD
NOTES

....

WEBSITE
USERNAME
PASSWORD
NOTES

WEBSITE
USERNAME
PASSWORD
NOTES

....

WEBSITE
USERNAME
PASSWORD
NOTES

....

WEBSITE
USERNAME
PASSWORD
NOTES

....

WEBSITE
USERNAME
PASSWORD
NOTES

WEBSITE
USERNAME
PASSWORD
NOTES

....
WEBSITE
USERNAME
PASSWORD
NOTES

....
WEBSITE
USERNAME
PASSWORD
NOTES

....
WEBSITE
USERNAME
PASSWORD
NOTES

WEBSITE
USERNAME
PASSWORD
NOTES

....

WEBSITE
USERNAME
PASSWORD
NOTES

....

WEBSITE
USERNAME
PASSWORD
NOTES

....

WEBSITE
USERNAME
PASSWORD
NOTES

WEBSITE
USERNAME
PASSWORD
NOTES

· ·

WEBSITE
USERNAME
PASSWORD
NOTES

· ·

WEBSITE
USERNAME
PASSWORD
NOTES

· ·

WEBSITE
USERNAME
PASSWORD
NOTES

WEBSITE
USERNAME
PASSWORD
NOTES

· ·

WEBSITE
USERNAME
PASSWORD
NOTES

· ·

WEBSITE
USERNAME
PASSWORD
NOTES

· ·

WEBSITE
USERNAME
PASSWORD
NOTES

WEBSITE

USERNAME

PASSWORD

NOTES

....

WEBSITE

USERNAME

PASSWORD

NOTES

....

WEBSITE

USERNAME

PASSWORD

NOTES

....

WEBSITE

USERNAME

PASSWORD

NOTES

WEBSITE
USERNAME
PASSWORD
NOTES

· ·

WEBSITE
USERNAME
PASSWORD
NOTES

· ·

WEBSITE
USERNAME
PASSWORD
NOTES

· ·

WEBSITE
USERNAME
PASSWORD
NOTES

WEBSITE

USERNAME

PASSWORD

NOTES

....

WEBSITE

USERNAME

PASSWORD

NOTES

....

WEBSITE

USERNAME

PASSWORD

NOTES

....

WEBSITE

USERNAME

PASSWORD

NOTES

WEBSITE
USERNAME
PASSWORD
NOTES

· ·

WEBSITE
USERNAME
PASSWORD
NOTES

· ·

WEBSITE
USERNAME
PASSWORD
NOTES

· ·

WEBSITE
USERNAME
PASSWORD
NOTES

WEBSITE

USERNAME

PASSWORD

NOTES

••

WEBSITE

USERNAME

PASSWORD

NOTES

••

WEBSITE

USERNAME

PASSWORD

NOTES

••

WEBSITE

USERNAME

PASSWORD

NOTES

WEBSITE
USERNAME
PASSWORD
NOTES

....

WEBSITE
USERNAME
PASSWORD
NOTES

....

WEBSITE
USERNAME
PASSWORD
NOTES

....

WEBSITE
USERNAME
PASSWORD
NOTES

WEBSITE
USERNAME
PASSWORD
NOTES

....

WEBSITE
USERNAME
PASSWORD
NOTES

....

WEBSITE
USERNAME
PASSWORD
NOTES

....

WEBSITE
USERNAME
PASSWORD
NOTES

WEBSITE
USERNAME
PASSWORD
NOTES

....

WEBSITE
USERNAME
PASSWORD
NOTES

....

WEBSITE
USERNAME
PASSWORD
NOTES

....

WEBSITE
USERNAME
PASSWORD
NOTES

WEBSITE

USERNAME

PASSWORD

NOTES

....

WEBSITE

USERNAME

PASSWORD

NOTES

....

WEBSITE

USERNAME

PASSWORD

NOTES

....

WEBSITE

USERNAME

PASSWORD

NOTES

WEBSITE
USERNAME
PASSWORD
NOTES

··
WEBSITE
USERNAME
PASSWORD
NOTES

··
WEBSITE
USERNAME
PASSWORD
NOTES

··
WEBSITE
USERNAME
PASSWORD
NOTES

WEBSITE

USERNAME

PASSWORD

NOTES

....

WEBSITE

USERNAME

PASSWORD

NOTES

....

WEBSITE

USERNAME

PASSWORD

NOTES

....

WEBSITE

USERNAME

PASSWORD

NOTES

WEBSITE

USERNAME

PASSWORD

NOTES

···

WEBSITE

USERNAME

PASSWORD

NOTES

···

WEBSITE

USERNAME

PASSWORD

NOTES

···

WEBSITE

USERNAME

PASSWORD

NOTES

WEBSITE
USERNAME
PASSWORD
NOTES

••

WEBSITE
USERNAME
PASSWORD
NOTES

••

WEBSITE
USERNAME
PASSWORD
NOTES

••

WEBSITE
USERNAME
PASSWORD
NOTES

WEBSITE

USERNAME

PASSWORD

NOTES

....

WEBSITE

USERNAME

PASSWORD

NOTES

....

WEBSITE

USERNAME

PASSWORD

NOTES

....

WEBSITE

USERNAME

PASSWORD

NOTES

WEBSITE

USERNAME

PASSWORD

NOTES

....

WEBSITE

USERNAME

PASSWORD

NOTES

....

WEBSITE

USERNAME

PASSWORD

NOTES

....

WEBSITE

USERNAME

PASSWORD

NOTES

WEBSITE
USERNAME
PASSWORD
NOTES

• •

WEBSITE
USERNAME
PASSWORD
NOTES

• •

WEBSITE
USERNAME
PASSWORD
NOTES

• •

WEBSITE
USERNAME
PASSWORD
NOTES

WEBSITE
USERNAME
PASSWORD
NOTES

....
WEBSITE
USERNAME
PASSWORD
NOTES

....
WEBSITE
USERNAME
PASSWORD
NOTES

....
WEBSITE
USERNAME
PASSWORD
NOTES

WEBSITE
USERNAME
PASSWORD
NOTES

· ·

WEBSITE
USERNAME
PASSWORD
NOTES

· ·

WEBSITE
USERNAME
PASSWORD
NOTES

· ·

WEBSITE
USERNAME
PASSWORD
NOTES

WEBSITE
USERNAME
PASSWORD
NOTES

....

WEBSITE
USERNAME
PASSWORD
NOTES

....

WEBSITE
USERNAME
PASSWORD
NOTES

....

WEBSITE
USERNAME
PASSWORD
NOTES

WEBSITE
USERNAME
PASSWORD
NOTES

··

WEBSITE
USERNAME
PASSWORD
NOTES

··

WEBSITE
USERNAME
PASSWORD
NOTES

··

WEBSITE
USERNAME
PASSWORD
NOTES

WEBSITE
USERNAME
PASSWORD
NOTES

WEBSITE
USERNAME
PASSWORD
NOTES

WEBSITE
USERNAME
PASSWORD
NOTES

WEBSITE
USERNAME
PASSWORD
NOTES

WEBSITE

USERNAME

PASSWORD

NOTES

....

WEBSITE

USERNAME

PASSWORD

NOTES

....

WEBSITE

USERNAME

PASSWORD

NOTES

....

WEBSITE

USERNAME

PASSWORD

NOTES

WEBSITE
USERNAME
PASSWORD
NOTES

....

WEBSITE
USERNAME
PASSWORD
NOTES

....

WEBSITE
USERNAME
PASSWORD
NOTES

....

WEBSITE
USERNAME
PASSWORD
NOTES

WEBSITE
USERNAME
PASSWORD
NOTES

WEBSITE
USERNAME
PASSWORD
NOTES

WEBSITE
USERNAME
PASSWORD
NOTES

WEBSITE
USERNAME
PASSWORD
NOTES

WEBSITE
USERNAME
PASSWORD
NOTES

WEBSITE
USERNAME
PASSWORD
NOTES

WEBSITE
USERNAME
PASSWORD
NOTES

WEBSITE
USERNAME
PASSWORD
NOTES

WEBSITE
USERNAME
PASSWORD
NOTES

....

WEBSITE
USERNAME
PASSWORD
NOTES

....

WEBSITE
USERNAME
PASSWORD
NOTES

....

WEBSITE
USERNAME
PASSWORD
NOTES

WEBSITE
USERNAME
PASSWORD
NOTES

WEBSITE
USERNAME
PASSWORD
NOTES

WEBSITE
USERNAME
PASSWORD
NOTES

WEBSITE
USERNAME
PASSWORD
NOTES

WEBSITE
USERNAME
PASSWORD
NOTES

....

WEBSITE
USERNAME
PASSWORD
NOTES

....

WEBSITE
USERNAME
PASSWORD
NOTES

....

WEBSITE
USERNAME
PASSWORD
NOTES

WEBSITE
USERNAME
PASSWORD
NOTES

....
WEBSITE
USERNAME
PASSWORD
NOTES

....
WEBSITE
USERNAME
PASSWORD
NOTES

....
WEBSITE
USERNAME
PASSWORD
NOTES

WEBSITE
USERNAME
PASSWORD
NOTES

WEBSITE
USERNAME
PASSWORD
NOTES

WEBSITE
USERNAME
PASSWORD
NOTES

WEBSITE
USERNAME
PASSWORD
NOTES

WEBSITE

USERNAME

PASSWORD

NOTES

....

WEBSITE

USERNAME

PASSWORD

NOTES

....

WEBSITE

USERNAME

PASSWORD

NOTES

....

WEBSITE

USERNAME

PASSWORD

NOTES

WEBSITE
USERNAME
PASSWORD
NOTES

....

WEBSITE
USERNAME
PASSWORD
NOTES

....

WEBSITE
USERNAME
PASSWORD
NOTES

....

WEBSITE
USERNAME
PASSWORD
NOTES

WEBSITE
USERNAME
PASSWORD
NOTES

....

WEBSITE
USERNAME
PASSWORD
NOTES

....

WEBSITE
USERNAME
PASSWORD
NOTES

....

WEBSITE
USERNAME
PASSWORD
NOTES

WEBSITE
USERNAME
PASSWORD
NOTES

....

WEBSITE
USERNAME
PASSWORD
NOTES

....

WEBSITE
USERNAME
PASSWORD
NOTES

....

WEBSITE
USERNAME
PASSWORD
NOTES

WEBSITE
USERNAME
PASSWORD
NOTES

....

WEBSITE
USERNAME
PASSWORD
NOTES

....

WEBSITE
USERNAME
PASSWORD
NOTES

....

WEBSITE
USERNAME
PASSWORD
NOTES

WEBSITE
USERNAME
PASSWORD
NOTES

....

WEBSITE
USERNAME
PASSWORD
NOTES

....

WEBSITE
USERNAME
PASSWORD
NOTES

....

WEBSITE
USERNAME
PASSWORD
NOTES

WEBSITE
USERNAME
PASSWORD
NOTES

••

WEBSITE
USERNAME
PASSWORD
NOTES

••

WEBSITE
USERNAME
PASSWORD
NOTES

••

WEBSITE
USERNAME
PASSWORD
NOTES

WEBSITE
USERNAME
PASSWORD
NOTES

• •

WEBSITE
USERNAME
PASSWORD
NOTES

• •

WEBSITE
USERNAME
PASSWORD
NOTES

• •

WEBSITE
USERNAME
PASSWORD
NOTES

WEBSITE

USERNAME

PASSWORD

NOTES

....

WEBSITE

USERNAME

PASSWORD

NOTES

....

WEBSITE

USERNAME

PASSWORD

NOTES

....

WEBSITE

USERNAME

PASSWORD

NOTES

WEBSITE
USERNAME
PASSWORD
NOTES

••

WEBSITE
USERNAME
PASSWORD
NOTES

••

WEBSITE
USERNAME
PASSWORD
NOTES

••

WEBSITE
USERNAME
PASSWORD
NOTES

WEBSITE
USERNAME
PASSWORD
NOTES

....

WEBSITE
USERNAME
PASSWORD
NOTES

....

WEBSITE
USERNAME
PASSWORD
NOTES

....

WEBSITE
USERNAME
PASSWORD
NOTES

WEBSITE
USERNAME
PASSWORD
NOTES

....

WEBSITE
USERNAME
PASSWORD
NOTES

....

WEBSITE
USERNAME
PASSWORD
NOTES

....

WEBSITE
USERNAME
PASSWORD
NOTES

Made in the USA
Las Vegas, NV
28 August 2024

94559002R00059